ID0429551

Simple
Wisdom

Illustrated by Roxana Villa

RUNNING PRESS
PHILADELPHIA · LONDON

A Running Press Miniature Edition™

© 1997 by Running Press
Illustrations © 1997 by Roxana Villa

All rights reserved under the Pan-American and International Copyright Conventions

Printed in China

Library of Congress Cataloging-in-Publication Number 96-71126

ISBN 0-7624-0197-4

This book may be ordered by mail from the publisher. Please include $1.00 for postage and handling. *But try your bookstore first!*

Running Press Book Publishers
125 South Twenty-second Street
Philadelphia, Pennsylvania 19103-4399

Contents

Introduction

People, both distinguished and plain, have been speaking words of wisdom since the dawn of civilization. It is what separates us from all other life on this planet.

Here is a collection of provocative thoughts from artists, writers, philosophers, and pop-culture icons from around the globe and across the ages. From Greek dramatist Euripides on suffering to TV's Andy Rooney on friendship, the myriad voices in this book speak to issues that we each face throughout our lives.

You will find that the essence of wisdom is simplicity; but it is elusive. It comes to those who experience life with eyes open and ears pricked. It can only enter an open mind that is attuned to its surroundings. Every glimpse of wisdom that you catch—whether on your own or through the help of others—shapes your view of the world.

The words and ideas in this book are meant to inspire self-reflection and meditation as you travel on your own path to wisdom.

CHAPTER ONE

Value

... from the sky, from the earth, from a scrap of paper, from a passing shape, from a spider's web.... We must pick out what is good for us where we can find it.

Pablo Picasso (1881–1973)
Spanish painter

Each moment of the year has its own beauty, a picture which was never seen before, and which shall never be seen again.

Ralph Waldo Emerson (1803–1882)
American essayist and philosopher

A little bit added

to what you've already got gives you

a little bit more.

P. G. Wodehouse (1881–1975)
English writer

Luxury need not have a price—
comfort itself is a luxury.

Geoffrey Beene (b. 1927)
American designer

I'd rather have

roses

on my table than

diamonds

on my neck.

Emma Goldman (1869–1940)
American anarchist

I love beautiful things; beauty in anything, beauty in an athlete, or just getting up very early in the morning for rehearsals.

Jessye Norman (b. 1945)
American opera singer

Cherish all your happy moments:
they make a fine cushion for old age.

Booth Tarkington (1869–1946)
American writer

Beauty is an ecstasy; it is as simple as hunger.

W. Somerset Maugham (1874–1965)
English writer

Style is
to see beauty in
modesty.

Andree Putnam
French Designer

A man's first care should be to avoid the reproaches of his own heart; his next, to escape the censures of the world.

Joseph Addison (1672–1719)
English writer

What right, what true, what fit
we justly call,
Let this be all my care—for this is all.

Horace (65–8 B.C.)
Roman poet

People exaggerate the value of things they haven't got.

George Bernard Shaw (1856–1950)
Irish-born playwright

What we obtain too cheap,
we esteem too lightly.

Thomas Paine (1737–1809)
American political philosopher

The good things
in life are like the birth of a child.
Ninety percent waiting.

James Michener (b. 1907)
American writer

To know is nothing at all;
to imagine is everything.

Anatole France Thibault (1844–1924)
French writer

CHAPTER TWO

Character

You can't depend on your judge-
ment when your imagination is
out of focus.

Mark Twain (1835–1910)
American writer

But if you have nothing at all to create, then perhaps you create yourself.

Carl Jung (1875–1961)
Swiss psychologist

Let your SOUL stand cool and composed before a million universes.

Walt Whitman (1819–1892)
American poet

For God's sake, choose a self
and stand by it.

William James (1842–1910)
American philosopher

It is possible to be
different and still be all right.

Anne Wilson Schaef
American writer

Let the world know you
as you are,

not as you think you should be.

Fanny Brice (1891–1951)
American singer

Follow your inner moonlight;

don't hide the madness.

Allen Ginsberg (b. 1926)
American poet

Ecstasy
is full, deep
involvement
in life.

John Lovell
American writer

How many cares one loses when one decides not to be something but to be someone.

Coco Chanel (1883–1971)
French fashion designer

Life engenders life. Energy creates energy. It is by spending oneself that one becomes rich.

Sarah Bernhardt (1844–1923)
French actress and writer

Plunge
boldly into the
thick of life.

Goethe (1749–1832)
German poet

Well-Being

'Tis folly only, and defect of sense
'Turns trifles into things
of consequence.

Martial (40–103)
Roman writer

Happiness is good health and a bad memory.

Ingrid Bergman (1915–1982)
Swedish-born actress

First
we have to
believe,
then we believe.

G. H. Lichtenberg (1742–1799)
German physicist

Perhaps our natural gifts elude

us because they are so obvious.

Sue Bender
American writer

To the question of your life, you
are the only answer.
To the problems of your life, you are
the only solution.

Jo Coudert
American TV executive

Infinite riches are all around you
if you will open your mental eyes and
behold the treasure house
of infinity within you.

Joseph Murphy
American writer

Nobody can conceive or imagine all the wonders there are unseen and unseeable in the world.

Francis P. Church
19th-century American writer

Miracles surround us

at every turn if we but sharpen our

perceptions of them.

Willa Cather (1873–1947)
American writer

It is always possible to approach
a goal by a detour.

Theodor Reik (1888–1969)
American psychologist

You see things; and you say "Why?"
But I dream things that never were;
and I say "Why not?"

George Bernard Shaw (1856–1950)
Irish-born playwright

Every spirit builds itself a house, and beyond its house a world, and beyond its world a heaven.

Ralph Waldo Emerson (1803–1882)
American essayist and philosopher

Put yourself into a different room,
that's what the mind is for.

Margaret Atwood (b. 1939)
Canadian writer and poet

If the doors of perception were cleansed, everything would appear as it is—infinite.

William Blake (1757–1827)
English poet

The truth is what is.
What *should be* is a dirty lie.

Lenny Bruce (1926–1966)
American comedian

Occasionally . . . what you have to do is go back to the beginning and see everything in a new way.

Peter Straub (b. 1943)
American writer

It's a very short trip.
While alive,
live!

Malcolm Forbes (1919–1990)
American publisher

I wish I had started out at the age
of 96. Look how much fun
I would have had.

Eubie Blake (1883–1983)
American musician

Success and Failure

I started with the firm conviction that when I came to the end, I wanted to be regretting the things that I *had* done, not the things I hadn't.

Michael Caine (b. 1933)
English actor

The greatest accomplishment is not in never falling, but in rising again after you fall.

Vince Lombardi (1913–1970)
American football coach

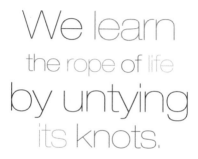

We learn
the rope of life
by untying
its knots.

Jean Toomer (1894–1967)
American writer

Every problem has a gift
for you in its hands.

Richard Bach
American writer

It is a relief when things get to their worst. You know what the worst is and can begin to plan for better things.

Elinore Pruitt Stewart (1878–1933)
American writer

Great minds must be ready not only to take opportunities, but to make them.

Charles Colton (1780–1832)
English clergyman

My challenge was not to do the impossible—but to learn to live with the possible.

Sue Bender
American writer

Falling short of perfection is a process that just never stops.

William Shawn (b. 1907)
American editor

Usefulness is not impaired by imperfection; you can drink from a chipped cup.

Greta K. Nagel
American writer

Perfectionism spells paralysis.

Winston Churchill (1874–1965)
English Prime Minister

There must be more to life

than having everything.

Maurice Sendak (b. 1928)
American writer

I always wanted to be a star—I'm not gonna bitch about it now.

Dolly Parton (b. 1946)
American entertainer

If there's one thing I know about destiny it is that you can't count on it forever.

Kinky Friedman
American writer

Keep your eyes open
and your mouth shut.

John Steinbeck (1902–1968)
American writer

Perspective

Since we cannot change reality, let us change the eyes that see reality.

Nikos Kazantzakis (1885–1957)
Greek writer

Your diamonds are not in far distant mountains or in yonder seas; they are in your own backyard, if you but dig for them.

Russell H. Conwell (1843–1925)
American minister

When you love
yourself,
you forgive
your own
imperfections.

Marilyn vos Savant (b. 1946)
American columnist

He better claims the glorious
name, who knows
With wisdom to enjoy what
heav'n bestows.

Horace (65–8 B.C.)
Roman poet

Look round the habitable world,
how few
Know their own good, or,
knowing it, pursue.

Juvenal (60–140)
Roman writer

Develop interest in life as you see it; in people, things, literature, music—the world is so rich, simply throbbing with rich treasures, beautiful souls and interesting people. Forget yourself.

Henry Miller (1891–1980)
American writer

In my apron, I carry nails, pliers,
a heavy hammer, and pride.

Moira Bachman
American labor activist

Work is not always required
. . . there is such a thing as
sacred idleness, the cultivation of which
is now fearfully neglected.

George MacDonald (1824–1905)
Scottish writer

The most revolutionary act
one can commit in our world is to
be happy.

Hunter "Patch" Adams
American physician

Living in balance and purity
is the highest good for you
and the earth.

Deepak Chopra (b. 1947)
Indian writer and physician

Life is the first gift, love is the second, and understanding, the third.

Marge Piercy (b. 1936)
American poet

Reverie is not a mind vacuum. It is rather the gift of an hour which knows the plentitude of the soul.

Gaston Bachelard (1884–1962)
French philosopher

Take the gentle path.

George Herbert (1593–1633)
English poet

The wise with hope

support the pains of life.

Euripides (484–407 B.C.)
Greek dramatist

My favorite thing is to
go where I've never been.

Diane Arbus (1923–1971)
American photographer

Where there is no hope,
there can be no endeavor.

Samuel Johnson (1709–1784)
English writer

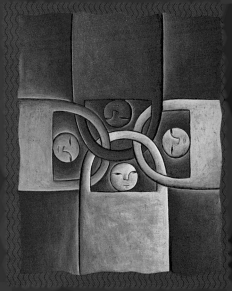

Relationships

The real marriage of true minds is for any two people to possess a sense of humor or irony pitched in exactly the same key.

Edith Wharton (1862–1937)
American writer and critic

I refuse to believe that trading recipes is silly. Tuna fish casserole is at least as real as corporate stock.

Barbara Grizzuti Harrison (b. 1941)
American writer

The person who tries to live alone
will not succeed as a human being.
The heart withers if it does not
answer another heart.

Pearl Buck (1892–1973)
American writer

Nowadays we are all of us so hard up that the only pleasant things to pay are compliments.

Oscar Wilde (1854–1900)
Irish writer

And we find at the end of a perfect day, the soul of a friend we've made.

Carrie Jacobs Bond (1862–1946)
American songwriter and composer

One of the sweetest things

in life: the letter from a friend.

Andy Rooney (b. 1919)
American journalist

Love is,
above all,
the gift of
oneself.

Jean Anouilh (1910–1987)
French playwright

Love is the spirit that motivates the artist's journey.

Eric Maisel
American artist

We are formed in important ways by
the love we feel in our hearts.

Ardath H. Rodale
American writer

You can't sweep people off their feet if you can't be swept off your own.

Clarence Day (1874–1935)
American writer

Love is not love until

love is vulnerable.

Theodore Roethke (1908–1963)
American poet

Freedom
is the spine
of love.

Sophia Loren (b. 1934)
Italian actress

Let there be spaces in your togetherness.

Kahlil Gibran (1883–1931)
Syrian-born American writer

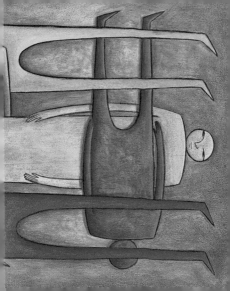

One word frees us of all the weight
and pain of life; that word is love.

Sophocles (495–406 B.C.)
Greek poet

You try to make an interesting journey between the cradle and the grave, you know?

Robert Duvall (b. 1931)
American actor

There is a vitality, a life force, an energy that is translated through you; and because there is only one you in all of time, this expression is unique.

Martha Graham (1894–1991)
American dancer

If it is your duty to croak like the toad, then go ahead! And with all your might! Make them hear you!

~~~~~~

Louis-Ferdinand Céline (1894–1961)
French writer

He lives to express himself,

and in so doing, enriches the world.

Henry Miller (1891–1980)
American writer